Elegant embossing with 3D

Else Plantinga

FORTE PUBLISHERS

Contents

© 2005 Forte Uitgevers, Utrecht
© 2005 for the translation by the publisher
Original title: *Sfeervol line embossing met 3D*

All rights reserved. No part of this publication may be copied, stored in an electronic file or made public, in any form or in any way whatsoever, either electronically, mechanically, by photocopying or any other form of recording, without the publisher's prior written permission.

ISBN 90 5877 515 1

This is a publication from
Forte Publishers BV
P.O. Box 1394
3500 BJ Utrecht
The Netherlands

For more information about the creative books available from Forte Uitgevers:
www.forteuitgevers.nl

Final editing: Gina Kors-Lambers, Steenwijk, the Netherlands
Photography and digital image editing: Fotografie Gerhard Witteveen, Apeldoorn, the Netherlands
Cover and inner design: BADE creatieve communicatie, Baarn, the Netherlands
Translation: Michael Ford, TextCase, Hilversum, the Netherlands

Preface	3
Techniques	4
Step-by-step	7
Materials	6
Elves	7
Dogs	11
Roses	15
Cats	19
Flowers	22
Marriage	25
Bears	28
Condolences	31

Preface

When I was asked to write a book about line embossing, I thought it would be a fun challenge.

There are seven line embossing templates, which I have combined with 3D and embroidery. Whilst I was making the cards, I noticed that there were many different possibilities. For example, I have dabbed some of the pictures with stamp-pad ink to highlight the effect.

The rose template, just like the other templates, can be used for 3D cutting. I am very pleased with the cards and hope that you will enjoy making them just as much as I did. You may even discover more possibilities with these line embossing templates.

Else

Techniques

3D cutting

To make a 3D picture, you need 3, 4 or sometimes 5 copies of the same picture. Various types of cuttings sheets have been used in this book. Cutting patterns are given for all the cards in this book, which show how many pictures you need to use and in which order they must be stuck on the card. The first picture is simply cut out and stuck on the card. The other layers are cut out and carefully shaped using a 3D shaping tool. Apply silicon glue to the back of the cut out pieces, turn them over and carefully stick them on the first picture. It is easier and makes less mess if you use a pair of tweezers to do this.

Embossing

Place the embossing template on the part of the card that you wish to emboss and stick it in place using non-permanent adhesive tape. Turn the template and the card over and place them on a light box. Use an embossing stylus to lightly press the lines of the embossing template to create a relief pattern in the card. Turn the template and the card over and use a sponge stick to apply ink to the embossed areas. Do not use too much ink. It is advisable to practise first on a piece of paper.

Embroidering

All the embroidery patterns are given in this book. Copy the embroidery pattern, use a piece of non-permanent adhesive tape to stick it where you wish to have the pattern and prick the holes. All the patterns are embroidered using the stem stitch. For this stitch, you first insert the needle through a hole, which is the first hole you count. You then insert the needle through the fourth hole. You then insert the needle through the second hole and then through the fifth hole, etc.

Step-by-step

1. The materials for line embossing.

2. Place the template on a light box and emboss the rose.

3. Dab stamp-pad ink on the rose.

4. Make the rose 3D.

Materials

- Card
- Line embossing stencils
- Embossing stylus
- Light box
- Colorbox inkpad
- Sponge sticks
- Perforating tool
- Pricking mat
- Sulky metallic embroidery thread
- Embroidery needle
- Cutting sheets
- 3D shaping tool
- Silicon glue and a syringe
- Knife
- Cutting mat
- Sticker sheets
- Adhesive stones
- Various punches
- Aleene's Tacky Glue

Pattern for the card "Sincere commiserations" (see page 32)

Cutting pattern for the card "Elf on a toadstool"

Elves

Elf on a toadstool

What you need
- Brilliant card: 175 g - silver blue (P162), 125 g - bronze (P164) and champagne (P163)
- Purple card
- Heart punch
- Fairyland cutting sheet
- Embossing template LE 2415
- Colorbox pinwheel inkpad
- Adhesive stones

Instructions
1. Make a double card (13.5 x 27 cm) and cut a purple card (12.5 x 12.5 cm), a silver blue card (12 x 12 cm) and a champagne card (6.5 x 12 cm).

2. Place the template on the silver blue card and stick it in place. Turn it over and place it on a light box

3. Use an embossing stylus to emboss the rose. Remove the template and the card from the light box, but leave the template and the card stuck together.

4. Use a number of different colours of stamp-pad ink to colour the rose.

5. Punch hearts in the champagne card.

6. Stick everything on the card.

7. Punch hearts out of a separate piece of purple card and stick them on the other punched out hearts.

8. Cut out the picture and make it 3D.

9. Use Tacky glue to stick adhesive stones on the rose.

Elf with a swan

What you need
- Mother-of-pearl paper: violet
- Perla card: 120 g - magnolia (P140)
- cArt-us card: violet
- Fairyland cutting sheet
- Embossing template LE 2419
- Sulky thread: metallic purple
- Sticker sheet: holographic border and flowers

Instructions
1. Make a double card (13.5 x 27 cm) and cut a magnolia card (11 x 11 cm).

2. Copy the embroidery pattern onto the card and use the stem stitch to embroider the pattern.

3. Place the template on the magnolia card and stick it in place. Turn it over and place it on a light box.

4. Copy the swan onto a separate piece of magnolia card and the hearts onto mother-of-pearl paper.

5. Use silicon glue to stick the swan and the hearts on the card.

6. Cut out the picture and make it 3D.

7. Decorate the card with decorative stickers.

Card with a mirror

What you need
- Brilliant card: champagne (P163)
- Mi-Teintes card: indigo
- Fairyland cutting sheet
- Round mirror
- Sulky thread: metallic silver/copper/blue and peacock blue
- Beads
- Embossing template LE2419
- Colorbox pinwheel inkpad

Instructions

1. Make a double card (13.5 x 27 cm) and cut an indigo card (13 x 13 cm) and a champagne card (12.5 x 12.5 cm).

2. Place the embroidery pattern on the champagne card and prick the pattern.

3. Use the stem stitch to embroider the pattern with two different colours of thread. Include some beads in the embroidery.

4. Place the template on a light box and emboss the birds. Use stamp-pad ink to colour the birds. Stick everything on the card.

5. Glue the mirror onto the card. Remove the protective cover on the mirror and glue the birds onto the mirror.

6. Cut out the picture and make it 3D.

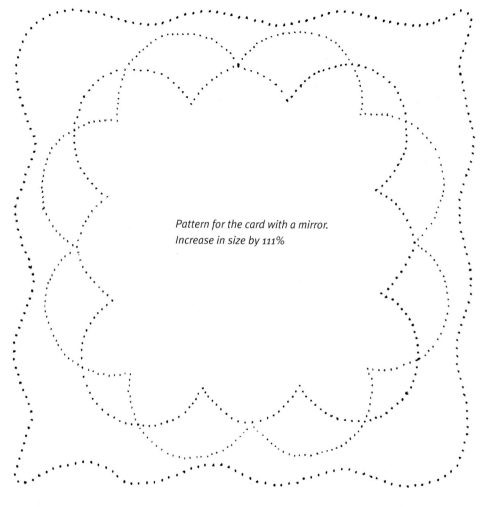

*Pattern for the card with a mirror.
Increase in size by 111%*

Pattern Elf with a swan

Dogs

Dog with a newspaper

What you need
- Ivory three window card
- Mi-Teintes card: sand and rust
- Embossing template LE 2418
- Sulky thread: metallic light copper
- Picturel cutting sheet: dogs
- Colorbox pinwheel inkpad

Instructions

1. Place a piece of sand card behind the openings in the card. Use a pencil to draw the squares so that you can see where you can emboss.

2. Place the template on the card and emboss two dogs and a food bowl. Use stamp-pad ink to colour the dogs and stick this inside the card.

3. Emboss the bows, cut them out and stick them in the corners of the openings in the card.

4. Use a pencil to copy four bones. Prick holes where you wish and embroider them.

5. Cut out the picture and make it 3D.

Dog with a ball

What you need
- *Mi-Teintes card: sand and dark wine red*
- *Picturel cutting sheet: dogs*
- *Sticker sheet: corners*
- *Embossing template LE2418*
- *Pigment marker pen*
- *Sulky thread: metallic copper red*
- *Colorbox pinwheel inkpad*

Instructions
1. Make a double card (13.5 x 27 cm) and cut a wine red (12.5 x 12.5 cm) and a sand card (12 x 12 cm).

2. Stick the template on the sand card. Turn it over, place it on a light box and emboss a line of three dogs, one under the other.

3. Turn the card and the template over and use stamp-pad ink to colour the dogs.

4. Place the pricking pattern on the card. Prick the pattern and embroider it using the stem stitch.

5. Cut out the dog and make it 3D.

6. Use the marker pen to colour the stickers and stick them above the embroidery.

Dog in a circle

What you need
- Mi-Teintes card: dark blue and lime
- Colorbox pinwheel inkpad
- Sulky thread: metallic peacock blue
- Picturel cutting sheet: dogs
- Sticker sheet: green/silver 1002

Instructions

1. Make a double card (13.5 x 27 cm) and cut a circle (Ø 12 cm).

2. Place the embroidery pattern on the card and prick the pattern.

3. Place the template on a light box and emboss the bone and the paws.

4. Use stamp-pad ink to colour the bone and the paws.

5. Use the stem stitch to embroider the pattern.

6. Cut out the circle and make it 3D.

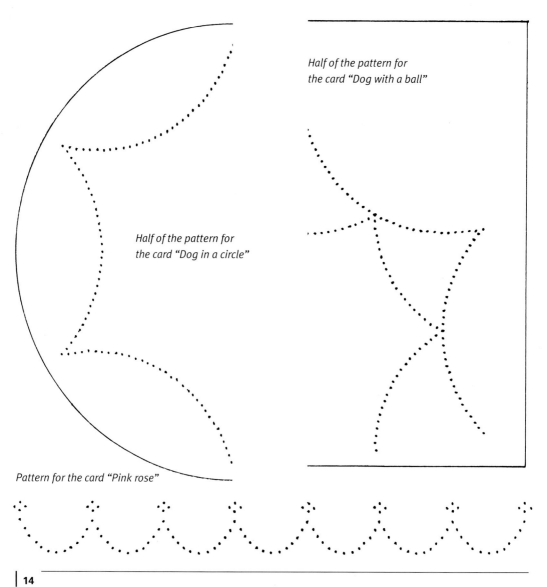

Roses

Pink rose

What you need
- Mi-Teintes card: violet and dawn
- Embossing template LE 2415
- Colorbox pinwheel inkpad
- Sulky thread: metallic lavender
- MD cutting sheet: Rosa
- Beads

Instructions
1. Make a double card (15 x 21 cm) and cut a violet card (7.5 x 11 cm).

2. Place the pattern on the card and prick the holes.

3. Place the template on a light box. Emboss the rose and use stamp-pad ink to colour it. Allow the ink to dry before starting the embroidery.

4. Use the stem stitch to embroider the pattern and include beads in the embroidery.

5. Cut out the rose. Stick it on violet card and stick this on the card. Make the rose 3D.

Light yellow rose

What you need
- cArt-us card: yellow
- Brilliant card: 125 g - champagne (P163)
- Embossing template LE 2415
- MD cutting sheet: Rosa
- Colorbox pinwheel inkpad
- Sulky thread: metallic gold
- Beads
- Holographic sticker sheet

Instructions

1. Make a double card (13.5 x 27 cm) and cut a champagne card (12.5 x 12.5 cm).

2. Place the template on a light box. Emboss the rose once on the champagne square and twice on a separate piece of champagne card, so that you can make the rose 3D later.

3. Use stamp-pad ink to colour the rose.

4. Prick the pattern in the card and use the stem stitch to embroider the pattern. Include some beads in the embroidery.

5. Stick the square on the yellow card.

6. Make the picture and the embossed rose 3D.

7. Stick a border sticker on the card.

1

2

3

4

Yellow rose

Instructions
1. Make a double card (15 x 21 cm) and cut a champagne card (4 x 15 cm).

2. Place the template on a light box. Emboss the rose on the champagne card and use stamp-pad ink to colour it.

3. Use the border punch to punch the border of the champagne card.

4. Prick the pattern in the card and use the stem stitch to embroider the pattern. Include some beads in the embroidery. Stick the champagne card on the card.

5. Make the rose 3D.

6. Stick the letters "Get well soon" on a piece of card. Stick a label sticker on it, cut the label out and use a cord to attach the label to the rose.

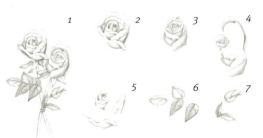

What you need
- cArt-us card: yellow
- Brilliant card: 125 g - champagne (P163)
- Colorbox pinwheel inkpad
- Border ornament punch: lace
- MD cutting sheet: Rosa
- Sulky thread: metallic gold
- Beads
- Embossing template LE2415
- Sticker sheet: labels

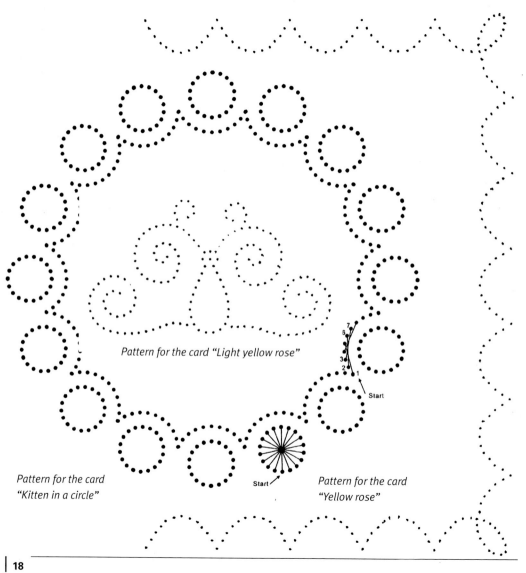

Kittens

Kitten in a circle

What you need
- Cardstock card: copper
- Brilliant card: 125 g - champagne (P163)
- Embossing template LE 2418
- Picturel cutting sheet: kittens
- Sulky thread: metallic silver/copper/blue
- Colorbox pinwheel inkpad

Instructions
1. Make a double card (13 x 26 cm).

2. Prick the pattern in the card and embroider it.

3. Place the template on a light box. Emboss the corners of the card and emboss the cat on the copper card. Use stamp-pad ink to colour the cat.

4. Cut a circle (Ø 7.5 cm) and stick it in the middle of the embroidery.

5. Make the cat on the circle 3D.

6. Glue the embossed cat onto the card.

Cut an incision

Cat with a car

Instructions
1. Make a double card (15 x 21 cm) and cut a silver card (15 x 10.5 cm).

2. Punch the border of the silver card.

3. Prick the pattern in the four sides and use the stem stitch to embroider them.

4. Emboss the cat basket on the silver card and stick this on the double card.

5. Emboss the cat on rust card and use silicon glue to stick it on the card.

6. Stick some adhesive stones on the punched border.

What you need
- Mi-Teintes card: rust
- Silver card
- Embossing templates LE 2418 and LE 2414
- Border ornament punch: sunflower
- Picturel cutting sheet: kittens
- Sulky thread: metallic silver/blue/pink
- Adhesive stones

Two cats

What you need
- Mi-Teintes card: rust
- Brilliant card: 125 g - champagne (P163)
- Embossing template LE 2414
- Mosaic ornament punch: star/lily
- Sulky thread: metallic silver/copper/blue
- Picturel cutting sheet: kittens

Instructions
1. Make a double card (13 x 26 cm).

2. Place the template on a light box. Emboss the frame on champagne card and punch the corners.

3. Prick the pattern in the corners of the card and use the stem stitch to embroider the pattern.

4. Stick the frame on the card

5. Stick the picture on the card and make it 3D.

1

2

3
Cut an incision

4

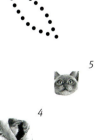
5

Flowers

Green card

What you need
- cArt-us card: dark green
- Mi-Teintes card: lime
- Embossing template LE 2413
- Picturel cutting sheet: bouquets
- Sulky thread: metallic silver/blue/pink and gold
- Adhesive stones

Instructions

1. Make a double card (15 x 21 cm).

2. Place the template on a light box. Emboss the frame on lime card and cut it out.

3. Prick the embroidery pattern in the card and the frame and use the stem stitch to embroider the pattern.

4. Glue the picture onto the card and stick the frame around it. Make the picture 3D. Glue adhesive stones onto the card and the frame.

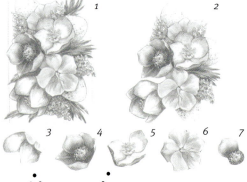

Yellow card

What you need
- cArt-us card: dark green and light yellow
- Embossing templates AE 1217 and LE 2413
- Sulky thread: metallic silver/red/jade
- Picturel cutting sheet: bouquets

Instructions

1. Make a double card (15 x 21 cm) and cut a dark green card (9.5 x 14 cm) and a yellow card (8 x 13 cm).

2. Emboss the pattern on the yellow rectangle.

3. Prick the pattern in the yellow rectangle and embroider it. Stick the yellow rectangle on the green rectangle and stick this on the card.

4. Emboss the pattern from template LE 2413 on a piece of green card. Cut it out and stick it in the embossed frame.

5. Make the flower 3D.

Blue card

What you need
- Mi-Teintes card: dark blue
- Brilliant card: champagne (P163)
- Embossing template LE 2416
- Sulky thread: metallic silver/blue/pink
- Beads
- Decorative frame K4-159-22
- Picturel cutting sheet: bouquets
- Colorbox pinwheel inkpad

Instructions
1. Make a double card (15 x 21cm).

2. Place the frame on the champagne card. Draw around the frame and cut it out. Cut a rectangle (4 x 8 cm) out of the middle of the frame.

3. Prick the pattern in the frame and embroider it. Include some beads in the embroidery.

4. Stick the frame on the card and stick the rectangle in the middle. Stick the picture on the card and make it 3D.

5. Emboss the butterfly twice on champagne card and use stamp-pad ink to colour it.

6. Stick the butterfly on the card. Cut out an extra wing and use silicon glue to stick it on the butterfly.

Marriage

Doves and hearts

What you need
- Silver card
- Brilliant card: 125 g - silver blue (P162)
- Embossing template LE2419
- Sulky thread: metallic dark pink
- Picturel step-by-step cutting sheet: marriage
- Adhesive stones
- Colorbox pinwheel inkpad

Instructions

1. Make a double card (15 x 21 cm).

2. Prick the pattern and embroider it.

3. Place the template on a light box. Emboss the bells and the bird on silver blue card and use stamp-pad ink to colour them.

4. Cut out the embossed shapes and stick the bells in the middle of the hearts.

5. Make the picture 3D and use silicon glue to stick the bird on the picture. Use Tacky glue to stick adhesive stones on the hearts.

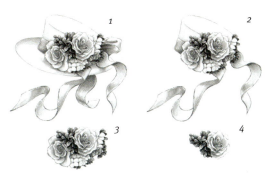

Wedding cake

Instructions

1. Make a double card (13 x 26 cm).

2. Place template AE 1217 on a light box. Emboss the rectangle so that you can cut it out later.

3. Place the other template on the light box. Emboss the cake once on the card and once on a piece of light pink card. Colour the cake on the separate piece of card and cut it out.

4. Place the pattern on the card. Prick two hearts and embroider them.

5. Stick the picture on the card and make it 3D.

6. Use silicon glue to stick the extra cake on the card.

7. Stick adhesive stones on the hearts.

What you need
- Mi-Teintes card: light pink
- Embossing template LE 2419
- Sulky thread: metallic dark pink
- Embossing template AE1217
- Picturel step-by-step cutting sheet: marriage
- Adhesive stones
- Colorbox pinwheel inkpad

Card with a hat

What you need
- Mi-Teintes card: light pink
- Silver card
- Picturel step-by-step cutting sheet: marriag
- Embossing template LE 2419
- Adhesive stones
- Sulky thread: metallic dark pink
- Colorbox pinwheel inkpad
- Border ornament punch: sunflower

Instructions
1. Make a double card (13 x 26 cm) and cut a silver rectangle (8.5 x 15 cm).

2. Punch the border of the rectangle and emboss the hat and the flowers. Stick it on the card.

3. Prick the pattern in the card and embroider the hearts.

4. Emboss the bottles on the side of the card and use stamp-pad ink to colour them.

5. Stick the picture on the card and make it 3D.

6. Use silicon glue to stick the hat on the card and stick adhesive stones on the hearts and in the punched border.

Bears

Pink bear card

What you need
- Mi-Teintes card: dawn and pink
- Sulky thread: metallic lavender
- Embossing template LE 2417
- Carré template C13
- Picturel cutting sheet: teddy bears

Instructions
1. Make a double card (13 x 26 cm).

2. Place the Carré template in each corner and emboss the shape.

3. Prick and embroider the pattern in the corners.

4. Cut out the middle of the card and glue light pink card behind the opening.

5. Emboss the stork twice on pink card and emboss the nappy and the hat on dawn card.

6. Stick the stork on the card and make it 3D.

7. Stick the picture on the card and make it 3D.

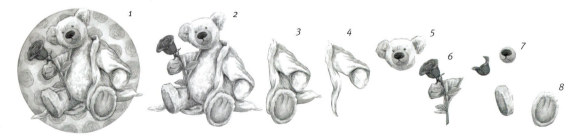

Light blue card

Instructions
1. Make a double card (15 x 21 cm).

2. Place the embroidery pattern at an angle on the card and prick the pattern. Use the stem stitch to embroider the pattern. Include some beads in the embroidery.

3. Place the template on a light box. Place the card on it at an angle and copy some of the shapes. Repeat this on a separate piece of card so that the shapes can be made 3D.

4. Stick the picture on the card and make it 3D.

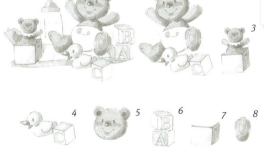

What you need
- Mi-Teintes card: azure
- Mini 3D cutting sheet: baby
- Embossing template LE 2417
- Sulky thread: metallic peacock blue
- Beads

Dark blue card

What you need
- Mi-Teintes card: dark blue and azure
- Mother-of-pear paper: white
- Sulky thread: white metallic prism
- Embossing template LE 2417
- Quadrant embossing template: Christmas tree
- Picturel cutting sheet: teddy bears

Instructions

1. Make a double card (15 x 21 cm).

2. Emboss the stork twice on azure card and cut them out.

3. Place the template on the card. Copy the moon and the stars and cut them out.

4. Place the embroidery template in the corners, prick the pattern and use the stem stitch to embroider the patterns.

5. Stick the stork and the picture on the card and make them 3D.

6. Stick a piece of mother-of-pearl paper inside the card.

Condolences

Condolences

What you need
- Mi-Teintes card: black
- Card: metallic mother-of-pearl and silver
- Sulky thread: metallic silver
- Sticker sheet: condolences
- Embossing template LE2416
- Silver beads
- Nel van Veen 3D cutting sheet: roses
- Holographic border sticker sheet

Instructions
1. Make a double card (15 x 21 cm) and cut a white card (10 x 15 cm), a black card (9 x 13.5 cm) and a silver card (8 x 12.5 cm).

2. Copy and prick the pattern and embroider it using the stem stitch.

3. Stick all of the rectangular cards onto the double card and stick the cross on top.

4. Cut out the rose and make it 3D.

5. Stick a border sticker around the card.

Sincere commiserations

Instructions
1. Make a double card (15 x 21 cm) and cut a white diamond shape.

2. Stick the diamond on the card.

3. Copy the pattern on page 6, place it in the corners and prick and embroider the pattern.

4. Place the template on a light box. Place a piece of white card on top and emboss the cross twice.

5. Use silicon glue to stick the cross on the diamond.

6. Stick the picture on the card and make it 3D.

7. Stick border stickers around the diamond.

What you need
- Mi-Teintes card: black
- Mother-of-pearl card: metallic white
- Holographic border sticker sheet
- Nel van Veen 3D cutting sheet: roses
- Sulky thread: metallic silver
- Embossing template LE2416

Many thanks to Papicolor International B.V. in Utrecht, the Netherlands, Avec B.V. in Waalwijk, the Netherlands, Kars en Co B.V. in Ochten, the Netherlands, Else Plantinga Design and De Hobbyzolder in Venhuizen, the Netherlands for providing the materials.
If you are not able to find some of the materials, contact De Hobbyzolder in Venhuizen, the Netherlands (+31 (0)228 544244) or see www.dehobbyzolder.nl for more information. There is a fan club for Else at www.clubs.nl